VEGETARIAN THAI COOKBOOK

70 Recipes for Asian Foods from Thailand

By

Maki Blanc

The trademarks that are used are without any consent, and the publication of the trademark is without permission or backing by the trademark owner. All trademarks and brands within this book are for clarifying purposes only and are owned by the owners themselves, not affiliated with this document.

Contents

CHAPTER 3: THE WORLD OF VEGETARIAN THAI DINNER RECIPES

Introduction

Thai food culture is very famous for its stunning food choices and amazing taste. The good contains sweet, spicy, sour and salty taste in a single bite. Food is loved a lot and the Thai people are huge fans of healthy and nutritious food.

Vegetarian foods are eaten all across the globe. People usually adopt the vegetarian diet for religious or personal reasons. Some People usually think that vegetarian foods may not taste as good as non-vegetarian foods but the vegetarian Thai food would change your perspective related to this thought.

From cooked vegetable sautés to hand beaten servings of mixed greens, you will be in heaven if you love cooking as well as eating with the assortment and proportion of food in the Thai cooking style given in this book. You will get in excess of 70 assorted vegetarian recipes. The recipes include vegetarian breakfast recipes, vegetarian lunch recipes, vegetarian dinner recipes, vegetarian dessert recipes, and vegetarian snack recipes that you can without a doubt start cooking at home with the definite instructions present underneath each recipe plan.

Setting up your simple Thai food at home without the need to arrange food from some eateries can turn out to be exceptionally simple once you begin perusing this book. Anyway, why sit tight and wait? Allow yourself to dive into the universe of Thai food.

Chapter 1: The World of Vegetarian Thai Breakfast Recipes

You have saved time, cash and calories by skipping your favorite Thai cafés and cooking by yourself at home. In this chapter you will learn some amazing Thai vegetarian breakfast dishes that you can easily make at home on your own.

1.1 Pak Boong Recipe

Preparation Time: 20 minutes

Cooking Time: 20 minutes

Serving: 4

Ingredients:

- Oyster sauce, one tablespoon
- Fresh Thai chili peppers, two
- Korean soybean paste, one tablespoon
- Sugar, half tablespoon
- Mirim, one tablespoon
- Soy sauce, half tablespoon
- Minced garlic, two teaspoon
- Cooking oil, three tablespoon
- Morning glory, two cups
- Salt, as required

- Chopped fresh cilantro, as required

Instructions:

1. Take a large pan.
2. Add the cooking oil into the pan and heat it.
3. Add the morning glory into the pan and stir-fry it.
4. Add the minced garlic along with the morning glory.
5. Cook your ingredients for five minutes until the color of the morning glory changes.
6. Add the soy sauce, mirim, sugar, fresh Thai chili peppers, Korean soy bean paste and oyster sauce into the mixture.
7. Cook your dish for ten minutes.
8. Dish out your pak boong and garnish it with chopped fresh cilantro leaves.
9. Your dish is ready to be served.

1.2 Thai Vegetarian Omelet Recipe

Preparation Time: 30 minutes

Cooking Time: 10 minutes

Serving: 4

Ingredients:

- Mushrooms, two
- Onions, half cup
- Rice wine, one tablespoon
- Black pepper, to taste
- Salt, to taste
- Starch, a quarter teaspoon
- Kohlrabi, one cup
- Ginger, one slice
- Soy sauce, one tablespoon
- Oil, one tablespoon
- Cilantro, as required

Instructions:

1. Beat the eggs with water, black pepper and salt.
2. Add oil to a wok, and then add the beaten eggs.
3. Sprinkle the vegetables on top.
4. Add the rest of the ingredients on top of your egg mixture.
5. Fold the egg and then cook it on both sides.
6. When the eggs are done, dish them out.

7. Add on top of the eggs the chopped cilantro leaves.

8. Your dish is ready to be served.

1.3 Thai Rice Congee Recipe

Preparation Time: 20 minutes

Cooking Time: 20 minutes

Serving: 2

Ingredients:

- Rice, one cup
- Cream, two tablespoon
- Butter, one cup
- Eggs, two
- Cherries, two
- All-purpose flour, two cups
- Water, as required
- Baking soda, one tablespoon
- Salt, a pinch
- Pepper, to taste

Instructions:

1. Take a large pan and clean it well.

2. Add the sugar and the baking soda and the rice into it.

3. Add the salt and the cream.

4. Add all-purpose flour into it so that congee can be smooth.

5. Add the crushed walnuts into the mixture.

6. Mix all the ingredients well.

7. Add beaten eggs into the mixture.

8. Pour into the dish and spread evenly.

9. Take a small bowl and add the butter.

10. Mix them until the mixture becomes smooth and then add it into your dish.

11. Add the salt as required.

12. Simmer it for about five minutes.

13. Your dish is ready to be served with cherries and the walnuts.

14. You can refrigerate your dish as well.

1.4 Thai Tofu Omelet Recipe

Preparation Time: 30 minutes

Cooking Time: 10 minutes

Serving: 4

Ingredients:

- Chopped tofu, one cup
- Red chili paste, two tablespoon
- Mushrooms, two

- Onions, half cup
- Eggs, four
- Rice wine, one tablespoon
- Black pepper, to taste
- Salt, to taste
- Green chilies, a quarter teaspoon
- Ginger, one slice
- Soy sauce, one tablespoon
- Oil, one tablespoon
- Cilantro, as required

Instructions:

1. Beat the eggs with the red wine, black pepper and salt.
2. Add oil to a large pan, and then add the beaten eggs.
3. Sprinkle the vegetables on top.
4. Add the chopped tofu on top of your mixture.
5. Add the rest of the ingredients on top of your egg mixture.
6. Fold the egg and then cook it on both sides.
7. When the eggs are done, dish them out.
8. Add on top of the eggs the chopped cilantro leaves.
9. Your dish is ready to be served.

1.5 Thai Black Rice Porridge Recipe

Preparation Time: 20 minutes

Cooking Time: 20 minutes

Serving: 2

Ingredients:

- Fish sauce, three teaspoon
- Cooked black rice, two cups
- Vegetable broth, one cup
- Cilantro, one tablespoon
- Black pepper, to taste
- Egg white, half cup
- Galangal, one slice
- Ginger, two tablespoon
- Palm sugar, one tablespoon
- Lime juice, one tablespoon
- Alfa one rice bran oil, teaspoon
- Coconut milk, one cup
- Bean sprouts, one cup
- Fried shallots, to serve
- Red chili, to serve

Instructions:

1. Cook the black rice in rice cooker.
2. Add the coconut milk into the mixture.

3. Boil the coconut milk along with mixture.

4. Continue boiling for five minutes until water reduces to minimum level.

5. Add the egg white and mix well.

6. Then take the vegetable broth in separate large pot.

7. Add the lemon grass and galangal in it.

8. Simmer it for five minutes.

9. Then add them in already cooked black rice.

10. Adjust taste by adding pepper and salt.

11. Your porridge is ready to be served.

12. Serve it with chilies and soy sauce.

1.6 Vegetarian Thai Egg and Chili Recipe

Preparation Time: 30 minutes

Cooking Time: 10 minutes

Serving: 4

Ingredients:

- Sugar, two teaspoon
- Fresh Thai chilies, four
- Eggs, four
- White pepper, a quarter teaspoon
- Water, half cup
- Scallions, one
- Sesame oil, two teaspoon

- Vegetable oil, three tablespoon

Instructions:

1. Heat the wok and add the oil.
2. Add the eggs and mix them.
3. Remove the scrambled eggs into a dish.
4. Add one more tablespoon of oil to the wok, and add the Thai chilies and scallions.
5. Stir-fry for one minute, and then add two teaspoons sugar, half teaspoon salt, and a quarter cup water.
6. Add the cooked eggs in the mixture.
7. Your dish is ready to be served.

1.7 Spicy Thai Kale and Coconut Fried Rice Recipe

Preparation Time: 30 minutes

Cooking Time: 10 minutes

Serving: 4

Ingredients:

- Sliced kale, one cup
- Shredded unsweetened coconut, half cup
- Red chilies, two
- Coconut milk, one cup
- Sliced green onions, half cup
- White peppercorns, one teaspoon
- Cilantro, one cup
- Fresh ginger, one teaspoon
- Fish sauce, one tablespoon
- Soy sauce, one tablespoon
- Chili garlic sauce, two tablespoon
- Fresh cilantro leaves, half cup
- Fresh basil leaves, a quarter cup
- Vegetable broth, one can
- Minced lemon grass, one teaspoon
- Egg, one large
- Cooked rice, as required
-

Instructions:

1. Add all the ingredients of the curry into a wok.
2. Add the vegetable broth and sauces into the mixture.
3. Cook your dish for ten minutes.

4. Add the cooked rice into the mixture.

5. Mix the rice well and cook it for five minutes.

6. Add the egg into the wok by pushing the rest of the ingredients to a side.

7. Cook the egg and then mix the rest of the ingredients into it.

8. Add the sliced kale and shredded coconut.

9. Cook your dish for five more minutes.

10.   Add the cilantro into the dish.

11.   Mix your rice and then dish it out.

12.   Your dish is ready to be served.

1.8 Vegetarian Thai Coconut Milk Rice Porridge Recipe

Preparation Time: 20 minutes

Cooking Time: 20 minutes

Serving: 2

Ingredients:

- Fish sauce, three teaspoon

- Cooked white rice, two cups
- Cilantro, one tablespoon
- Black pepper, to taste
- Egg whites, half cup
- Galangal, one slice
- Ginger, two tablespoon
- Palm sugar, one tablespoon
- Lime juice, one tablespoon
- Alfa one rice bran oil, teaspoon
- Coconut milk, two cup
- Fried shallots, to serve
- Red chili, to serve

Instructions:

1. Cook the white rice in rice cooker.
2. Add the coconut milk into the mixture.
3. Boil the coconut milk along with mixture.
4. Continue boiling for five minutes until water reduces to minimum level.
5. Add the egg whites and mix well.
6. Add the lemon grass and galangal in it.
7. Simmer it for five minutes.
8. Then add them in already cooked white rice.
9. Adjust taste by adding pepper and salt.
10. Your porridge is ready to be served.

11.   Serve it with chilies and soy sauce.

1.9 Vegetarian Thai Omelet Soup Recipe

Preparation Time: 30 minutes

Cooking Time: 10 minutes

Serving: 4

Ingredients:

- Mushrooms, two
- Onions, half cup
- Rice wine, one tablespoon
- Black pepper, to taste
- Salt, to taste
- Starch, a quarter teaspoon
- Kohlrabi, one cup
- Ginger, one slice
- Soy sauce, one tablespoon
- Oil, one tablespoon
- Cilantro, as required

For soup:

- Vegetable stock, four cups
- Thai basil, half cup
- Salt, to taste
- Black pepper, to taste

- Lime juice, one tablespoon
- Thai red pepper, half teaspoon

Instructions:

1. Beat the eggs with water, black pepper and salt.
2. Add oil to a wok, and then add the beaten eggs.
3. Sprinkle the vegetables on top.
4. Add the rest of the ingredients on top of your egg mixture.
5. Fold the egg and then cook it on both sides.
6. When the eggs are done, dish them out.
7. In the wok, add the vegetable stock and the spices for the soup.
8. When the soup boils enough, add the omelet into the soup.
9. Cook your soup for five minutes.
10. Garnish your soup with the chopped cilantro leaves.
11. Your dish is ready to be served.

1.10 Thai Scrambled Tofu and Egg Recipe

Preparation Time: 30 minutes

Cooking Time: 10 minutes

Serving: 4

Ingredients:

- Butter, two tablespoon
- Coconut cream, half cup
- Chopped tofu, half pound
- Salt, to taste
- Southwest chili sauce, two tablespoon
- Black pepper, to taste
- Chopped fresh chives, as required
- Eggs, twelve
- Onions, one
- Chopped garlic, one teaspoon

Instructions:

1. In a large wok, add the butter and let it meltdown.
2. Add in the chopped onion.
3. Cook the onions until soft.
4. Add in the garlic.
5. Mix the onions and garlic for two minutes and add in the chopped tofu pieces.
6. Add the eggs and let it cook.
7. Scramble the mixture.
8. Add in the salt and pepper.
9. Add in the coconut cream in the end.
10. When the eggs are done, dish them out.
11. Add the fresh chopped chives on top.
12. Your dish is ready to be served.

1.11 Vegetarian Thai Rice Soup Recipe

Preparation Time: 30 minutes

Cooking Time: 10 minutes

Serving: 4

Ingredients:

- White peppercorns, one teaspoon
- Cilantro, one cup
- Ginger paste, two tablespoon
- Fish sauce, one tablespoon
- Soy sauce, one and a half tablespoon
- Vegetable stock, three cup
- Jasmine rice, four cups
- Garlic cloves, four

Instructions:

1. Crush the white peppercorns until they turn into powdered form.
2. At that point add garlic and cilantro and pound until they are crushed.
3. Season with fish sauce and soy sauce, at that point taste and add more if you prefer.
4. When prepared to serve, heat the stock to the point of boiling.

5. Add the rice into the stock.

6. Add the soup into a bowl.

7. Garnish it with cilantro leaves.

8. Your dish is ready to be served.

1.12 Vegetarian Thai Fried Rice Recipe

Preparation Time: 30 minutes

Cooking Time: 10 minutes

Serving: 4

Ingredients:

- Thai chilies, two
- Sliced green onions, half cup
- White peppercorns, one teaspoon
- Cilantro, one cup
- Fresh ginger, one teaspoon
- Fish sauce, one tablespoon
- Soy sauce, one tablespoon

- Chili garlic sauce, two tablespoon
- Fresh cilantro leaves, half cup
- Thai basil leaves, a quarter cup
- Mixed vegetables, one cup
- Cooked rice, as required

Instructions:

1. Heat a large pan.
2. Add the vegetable broth and sauces into the mixture.
3. Cook your dish for ten minutes.
4. Add the cooked rice into the mixture.
5. Mix the rice well and cook it for five minutes.
6. Add the mixed vegetable and rest of the ingredients into the mixture.
7. Cook your dish for five more minutes.
8. Add the cilantro into the dish.
9. Mix your rice and then dish it out.
10. Your dish is ready to be served.

Chapter 2: The World of Vegetarian Thai Lunch Recipes

Thai lunch recipes consist of amazing dishes that are healthy, nutritious and flavorful at the same time. Following are some amazing Thai lunch recipes that you can easily make at home:

2.1 Vegetarian Thai Coconut Soup Recipe

Preparation Time: 30 minutes

Cooking Time: 10 minutes

Serving: 4

Ingredients:

- Water, two cups
- Galangal, one can
- Minced garlic, one teaspoon
- Minced ginger, one teaspoon
- Chopped onion, half cup
- Minced ginger, half tablespoon
- Lemon grass, two sticks
- Fish sauce, two tablespoon
- Shredded coconut, one cup
- Coconut milk, one cup

- Cilantro, a quarter cup
- Olive oil, one tablespoon

Instructions:

1. Take a large sauce wok.
2. Add the chopped onion and olive oil.
3. Cook your chopped onion.
4. When the onions are cooked then add the galangal, garlic and ginger.
5. Add the coconut milk.
6. Cook your ingredients until they start boiling.
7. Add in the shredded coconut, lemon grass and rest of the ingredients into your soup.
8. Cook your ingredients for ten minutes.
9. Garnish it with cilantro leaves.
10. Your dish is ready to be served.

2.2 Vegetarian Thai Tomato Soup Recipe

Preparation Time: 30 minutes

Cooking Time: 10 minutes

Serving: 4

Ingredients:

- Galangal, one can
- Vegetable stock, two cups

- Minced garlic, one teaspoon

- Palm sugar, two tablespoon

- Shallot, one

- Kaffir lime leaves, four

- Lime wedges

- Chopped tomatoes, one cup

- Lemon grass, two sticks

- Fish sauce, two tablespoon

- Tomato puree, one cup

- Coconut milk, one cup

- Cilantro, a quarter cup

- Olive oil, one tablespoon

Instructions:

1. Take a large sauce pan.

2. Add the shallots and olive oil.

3. Add the galangal, vegetable stock, and minced garlic.

4. Cook your ingredients until they start boiling.

5. Add in the tomatoes, tomato puree, lemon grass and rest of the ingredients into your soup.

6. Cook your ingredients for ten minutes.

7. Garnish it with cilantro leaves.

8. Your dish is ready to be served.

2.3 Vegetarian Thai Creamy Red Lentil Curry Recipe

Preparation Time: 30 minutes

Cooking Time: 10 minutes

Serving: 4

Ingredients:

- Vegetable stock, two cups
- Minced garlic, one teaspoon
- Palm sugar, two tablespoon
- Coconut cream, one cup
- Shallot, one
- Kaffir lime leaves, four
- Lime wedges
- Lemon grass, two sticks
- Fish sauce, two tablespoon
- Coconut milk, one cup
- Cilantro, a quarter cup
- Red lentils, half pound
- Olive oil, one tablespoon

Instructions:

1. Take a large sauce pan.
2. Add the shallots and olive oil.
3. Cook your shallots and then add the red lentil.
4. When the red lentil is half cooked, add the vegetable stock, and minced garlic.
5. Add the palm sugar and coconut milk.
6. Cook your ingredients until they start boiling.
7. Add in the coconut cream and rest of the ingredients into your soup.
8. Cook your ingredients for ten minutes.
9. Garnish it with cilantro leaves.
10. Your dish is ready to be served.

2.4 Vegetarian Thai Chili Lime Noodles Recipe

Preparation Time: 30 minutes

Cooking Time: 10 minutes

Serving: 4

Ingredients:

- Mixed vegetables, two cups
- Sliced green onions, half cup
- White peppercorns, one teaspoon
- Cilantro, one cup
- Fresh ginger, one teaspoon

- Fish sauce, one tablespoon

- Soy sauce, one tablespoon

- Chili lime sauce, one cup

- Chili garlic sauce, two tablespoon

- Fresh cilantro leaves, half cup

- Fresh basil leaves, a quarter cup

- Vegetable broth, one cup

- Noodles, as required

Instructions:

1. Add all the ingredients of the sauce into a wok.

2. Add the chili lime sauce, mixed vegetables, vegetable broth and sauces into the mixture.

3. Cook your dish for ten minutes.

4. Add the noodles into the mixture once the sauce is ready.

5. Mix the noodles well and cook them for five minutes.

6. Add the cilantro into the dish.

7. Cook your noodles and then dish them out.

8. Your dish is ready to be served.

2.5 Vegetarian Thai Garlic and Broccoli Stir-Fry Recipe

Preparation Time: 10 minutes

Cooking Time: 20 minutes

Serving: 4

Ingredients:

- Fish sauce, two tablespoon
- Soy sauce, half cup
- Tomatoes, two
- Broccoli florets, two cups
- Cilantro, half cup
- Salt and pepper, to taste
- Minced ginger, half tablespoon
- Vegetable oil, two tablespoon
- Red chili peppers, three
- Onion, one
- Toasted nuts, half cups
- Scallions, half cup
- Minced garlic, one teaspoon

Instructions:

1. In a large wok, add the shallots and oil.

2. Cook your shallots and then add the ginger and garlic.

3. Cook your ginger and garlic.

4. Add the broccoli florets and the rest of the ingredients into your dish except the toasted nuts.

5. Cook your dish for five minutes.

6. Garnish your dish with cilantro.

7. Your dish is ready to be served.

2.6 Vegetarian Thai Cauliflower Curry Recipe

Preparation Time: 30 minutes

Cooking Time: 10 minutes

Serving: 4

Ingredients:

- Vegetable stock, two cups
- Minced garlic, one teaspoon
- Thai spices, two tablespoon
- Shallot, one
- Kaffir lime leaves, four
- Lime wedges
- Lemon grass, two sticks
- Fish sauce, two tablespoon
- Coconut milk, one cup

- Cilantro, a quarter cup

- Cauliflower florets, half pound

- Olive oil, one tablespoon

Instructions:

1. Take a large sauce pan.

2. Add the shallots and olive oil.

3. Cook your shallots and then add the cauliflower florets.

4. When the cauliflower florets are half cooked, add the vegetable stock, and minced garlic.

5. Add the coconut milk.

6. Cook your ingredients for ten minutes.

7. Garnish it with cilantro leaves.

8. Your dish is ready to be served.

2.7 Vegetarian Thai Quinoa Recipe

Preparation Time: 30 minutes

Cooking Time: 25 minutes

Serving: 4

Ingredients:

- Minced garlic, two tablespoon
- Minced ginger, two tablespoon
- Cilantro, half cup
- Olive oil, two tablespoon
- Chopped tomatoes, one cup
- Quinoa, one cup
- Turmeric powder, one teaspoon
- Onion, one cup
- Vegetable broth, one cup
- Smoked paprika, half teaspoon
- Water, one cup

Instructions:

1. Take a pan.
2. Add in the oil and onions.
3. Cook the onions until they become soft and fragrant.
4. Add in the chopped garlic and ginger.
5. Cook the mixture and add the tomatoes into it.
6. Add the spices.

7. When the tomatoes are done, add the quinoa into it.

8. Add in the broth.

9. Mix the ingredients carefully and cover your pan.

10. When your quinoa is done, add in the cilantro.

11. Mix the quinoa and let it cook for an additional five minutes.

12. Your dish is ready to be served.

2.8 Vegetarian Thai Red Butternut Squash Curry Recipe

Preparation Time: 30 minutes

Cooking Time: 10 minutes

Serving: 4

Ingredients:

- Thai red curry paste, one tablespoon
- Vegetable stock, two cups
- Minced garlic, one teaspoon
- Thai spices, two tablespoon
- Shallot, one
- Kaffir lime leaves, four
- Lime wedges
- Lemon grass, two sticks

- Fish sauce, two tablespoon

- Coconut milk, one cup

- Cilantro, a quarter cup

- Butternut squash pieces, half pound

- Olive oil, one tablespoon

Instructions:

1. Take a large sauce pan.

2. Add the shallots and olive oil.

3. Cook your shallots and then add the butternut squash pieces.

4. When the butternut squash pieces are half cooked, add the galangal, vegetable stock, and minced garlic.

5. Add the Thai red curry paste into your curry.

6. Add the coconut milk.

7. Cook your ingredients until it starts boiling.

8. Garnish it with cilantro leaves.

9. Your dish is ready to be served.

2.9 Vegetarian Thai Cashew Vegetables Recipe

Preparation Time: 30 minutes

Cooking Time: 10 minutes

Serving: 4

Ingredients:

- Mixed vegetables, two cups
- Sliced green onions, half cup
- White peppercorns, one teaspoon
- Cilantro, one cup
- Fresh ginger, one teaspoon
- Fish sauce, one tablespoon
- Soy sauce, one tablespoon
- Chili garlic sauce, two tablespoon
- Fresh cilantro leaves, half cup
- Fresh basil leaves, a quarter cup
- Vegetable broth, one cup
- Cashew nuts, one cup

Instructions:

1. Add all the ingredients of the sauce into a wok.
2. Add the mixed vegetables, vegetable broth and sauces into the mixture.
3. Cook your dish for ten minutes.
4. Add the cashew nuts into the mixture once the sauce is ready.

5. Mix the cashew nuts well and cook it for five minutes.

6. Add the cilantro into the dish.

7. Cook your cashew nuts and then dish it out.

8. Your dish is ready to be served.

2.10 Vegetarian Thai Vegetable and Potato Yellow Curry Recipe

Preparation Time: 30 minutes

Cooking Time: 10 minutes

Serving: 4

Ingredients:

- Yellow curry paste, two tablespoon
- Vegetable stock, two cups
- Minced garlic, one teaspoon
- Thai spices, two tablespoon
- Shallot, one
- Mixed vegetables, half cup
- Kaffir lime leaves, four
- Lime wedges
- Lemon grass, two sticks
- Fish sauce, two tablespoon
- Coconut milk, one cup
- Cilantro, a quarter cup
- Potatoes, half pound
- Olive oil, one tablespoon

Instructions:

1. Take a large sauce pan.

2. Add the shallots and olive oil.

3. Cook your shallots and then add the vegetables and potatoes.

4. Add the vegetable stock, and minced garlic.

5. Add the coconut milk.

6. Add the yellow curry paste and the rest of the ingredients.

7. Cook your ingredients for ten minutes.

8. Garnish it with cilantro leaves.

9. Your dish is ready to be served.

2.11 Vegetarian Thai Jackfruit and Potato Curry Recipe

Preparation Time: 30 minutes

Cooking Time: 10 minutes

Serving: 4

Ingredients:

- Jackfruit chunks, two cups

- Vegetable stock, two cups

- Minced garlic, one teaspoon

- Thai spices, two tablespoon

- Shallot, one

- Kaffir lime leaves, four
- Lime wedges
- Lemon grass, two sticks
- Fish sauce, two tablespoon
- Coconut milk, one cup
- Cilantro, a quarter cup
- Potatoes, half pound
- Olive oil, one tablespoon

Instructions:

1. Take a large sauce pan.
2. Add the shallots and olive oil.
3. Cook your shallots and then add the potatoes.
4. Add the vegetable stock, and minced garlic.
5. Add the coconut milk.
6. Add the jackfruit chunks and the rest of the ingredients.
7. Cook your ingredients for ten minutes.
8. Garnish it with cilantro leaves.
9. Your dish is ready to be served.

2.12 Vegetarian Thai Sweet Chili Tofu Recipe

Preparation Time: 30 minutes

Cooking Time: 10 minutes

Serving: 4

Ingredients:

- Mixed vegetables, two cups
- Sliced green onions, half cup
- White peppercorns, one teaspoon
- Cilantro, one cup
- Fresh ginger, one teaspoon
- Fish sauce, one tablespoon
- Soy sauce, one tablespoon
- Chili paste, one tablespoon
- Tofu cubes, two cup
- Chili garlic sauce, two tablespoon
- Fresh cilantro leaves, half cup
- Fresh basil leaves, a quarter cup
- Vegetable broth, one cup

Instructions:

1. Add all the ingredients of the sauce into a wok.

2. Add the chili paste, mixed vegetables, vegetable broth and sauces into the mixture.

3. Cook your dish for ten minutes.

4. Add the tofu cubes and the rest of the ingredients into the mixture once the sauce is ready.

5. Mix the tofu cubes well and cook it for five minutes.

6. Add the cilantro into the dish.

7. Your dish is ready to be served.

2.13 Vegetarian Thai Peanut and Chickpea Buddha Bowl Recipe

Preparation Time: 10 minutes

Cooking Time: 20 minutes

Serving: 4

Ingredients:

- Minced ginger, two tablespoon
- Lemon juice, half cup
- Cilantro, one cup
- Olive oil, two tablespoon
- Chopped tomatoes, one cup
- Wild rice, one cup

- Turmeric powder, one teaspoon

- Onion, one cup

- Peanuts, one cup

- Cooked chickpeas, one cup

- Smoked paprika, half teaspoon

- Chopped carrots, one cup

- Minced garlic, two tablespoon

Instructions:

1. Take a pan.

2. Add in the oil and onions.

3. Cook the onions until they become soft and fragrant.

4. Add in the chopped garlic and ginger.

5. Cook the mixture and add the tomatoes into it.

6. Add the spices.

7. When the tomatoes are done, add the chickpeas into it.

8. Mix the ingredients carefully and place your mixture into the oven.

9. When your chickpeas are done, dish them out.

10. In a bowl, place the chickpeas with the peanuts.

11. Add cilantro on top.

12. Your dish is ready to be served.

2.14 Vegetarian Thai Chickpea and Coconut Rice Recipe

Preparation Time: 30 minutes

Cooking Time: 10 minutes

Serving: 4

Ingredients:

- Thai chilies, two
- Sliced green onions, half cup
- White peppercorns, one teaspoon
- Cilantro, one cup
- Fresh ginger, one teaspoon
- Fish sauce, one tablespoon
- Soy sauce, one tablespoon
- Shredded coconut, two tablespoon
- Fresh cilantro leaves, half cup
- Thai basil leaves, a quarter cup
- Cooked chickpeas, one cup
- Cooked rice, as required

Instructions:

1. Heat a large pan.
2. Add the vegetable broth and sauces into the mixture.
3. Cook your dish for ten minutes.

4. Add the cooked rice into the mixture.

5. Mix the rice well and cook it for five minutes.

6. Add the cooked chickpeas and rest of the ingredients into the mixture.

7. Cook your dish for five more minutes.

8. Add the cilantro into the dish.

9. Mix your rice and then dish it out.

10. Your dish is ready to be served.

2.15 Vegetarian Thai Black Pepper Greens and Tofu Curry Recipe

Preparation Time: 30 minutes

Cooking Time: 10 minutes

Serving: 4

Ingredients:

- Vegetable stock, two cups
- Minced garlic, one teaspoon
- Thai spices, two tablespoon
- Shallot, one
- Kaffir lime leaves, four
- Green vegetables, two cups
- Lemon grass, two sticks
- Fish sauce, two tablespoon
- Black pepper, two teaspoon

- Coconut milk, one cup

- Cilantro, a quarter cup

- Tofu cubes, half pound

- Olive oil, one tablespoon

Instructions:

1. Take a large sauce pan.
2. Add the shallots and olive oil.
3. Cook your shallots and then add the greens and tofu cubes.
4. When the ingredients are half cooked, add the vegetable stock, and minced garlic.
5. Add the coconut milk.
6. Add all the rest of the ingredients.
7. Cook your ingredients for ten minutes.
8. Garnish it with cilantro leaves.
9. Your dish is ready to be served.

Chapter 3: The World of Vegetarian Thai Dinner Recipes

This Chapter contains those yummy Thai dinner recipes that you have been longing to make in your kitchen.

3.1 Vegetarian Thai Yellow Tofu Curry Recipe

Preparation Time: 30 minutes

Cooking Time: 10 minutes

Serving: 4

Ingredients:

- Yellow curry paste, two tablespoon
- Vegetable stock, two cups
- Minced garlic, one teaspoon
- Thai spices, two tablespoon
- Shallot, one
- Galangal, half teaspoon
- Mixed vegetables, half cup
- Kaffir lime leaves, four
- Lemon grass, two sticks
- Fish sauce, two tablespoon

- Coconut milk, one cup
- Cilantro, a quarter cup
- Tofu cubes, half pound
- Olive oil, one tablespoon

Instructions:

1. Take a large sauce pan.

2. Add the shallots and olive oil.

3. Cook your shallots and then add the vegetables and tofu cubes.

4. Add the galangal, vegetable stock, and minced garlic.

5. Add the coconut milk.

6. Add the yellow curry paste and the rest of the ingredients.

7. Cook your ingredients for ten minutes.

8. Garnish it with cilantro leaves.

9. Your dish is ready to be served.

3.2 Vegetarian Thai Potato, Spinach and Chickpea Curry Recipe

Preparation Time: 30 minutes

Cooking Time: 10 minutes

Serving: 4

Ingredients:

- Vegetable stock, two cups
- Minced garlic, one teaspoon
- Thai spices, two tablespoon
- Shallot, one
- Kaffir lime leaves, four
- Spinach, two cup
- Lemon grass, two sticks
- Fish sauce, two tablespoon
- Potato cubes, two cups
- Galangal, half teaspoon
- Coconut milk, one cup
- Cilantro, a quarter cup
- Chickpeas, half pound
- Olive oil, one tablespoon

Instructions:

1. Take a large sauce pan.
2. Add the shallots and olive oil.

3. Cook your shallots and then add the chickpeas and potatoes.

4. When the ingredients are half cooked, add the galangal, vegetable stock, and minced garlic.

5. Add the coconut milk.

6. Add the spinach and all the rest of the ingredients.

7. Cook your ingredients for ten minutes.

8. Garnish it with cilantro leaves.

9. Your dish is ready to be served.

3.3 Vegetarian Thai Massaman Curry Recipe

Preparation Time: 30 minutes

Cooking Time: 25 minutes

Serving: 4

Ingredients:

- Minced garlic, two tablespoon
- Minced ginger, two tablespoon
- Cilantro, half cup
- Olive oil, two tablespoon
- Chopped tomatoes, one cup
- Massaman, one cup
- Turmeric powder, one teaspoon
- Onion, one cup

- Vegetable broth, one cup

- Smoked paprika, half teaspoon

- Water, one cup

Instructions:

1. Take a pan.

2. Add in the oil and onions.

3. Cook the onions until they become soft and fragrant.

4. Add in the chopped garlic and ginger.

5. Cook the mixture and add the tomatoes into it.

6. Add the spices.

7. When the tomatoes are done, add the quinoa into it.

8. Add in the broth.

9. Mix the ingredients carefully and cover your pan.

10. When your massaman is done, add in the cilantro.

11. Mix your massaman and let it cook for an additional five minutes.

12. Your dish is ready to be served.

3.4 Vegetarian Thai Pumpkin Curry Recipe

Preparation Time: 30 minutes

Cooking Time: 10 minutes

Serving: 4

Ingredients:

- Vegetable stock, two cups
- Minced garlic, one teaspoon
- Thai spices, two tablespoon
- Shallot, one
- Kaffir lime leaves, four
- Lime wedges
- Lemon grass, two sticks
- Fish sauce, two tablespoon
- Coconut milk, one cup
- Cilantro, a quarter cup
- Pumpkin pieces, half pound
- Olive oil, one tablespoon

Instructions:

1. Take a large sauce pan.
2. Add the shallots and olive oil.
3. Cook your shallots and then add the pumpkin pieces.
4. When the pumpkin pieces are half cooked, add the vegetable stock, and minced garlic.
5. Add the coconut milk and rest of the ingredients.
6. Cook your ingredients for ten minutes.
7. Garnish it with cilantro leaves.

8. Your dish is ready to be served.

3.5 Vegetarian Thai Baked Tofu with Noodles Recipe

Preparation Time: 10 minutes

Cooking Time: 20 minutes

Serving: 4

Ingredients:

- Powdered cumin, one tablespoon
- Salt, to taste
- Black pepper, to taste
- Turmeric powder, one teaspoon
- Onion, one cup
- Vegetable broth, one cup
- Smoked paprika, half teaspoon
- Dijon mustard, half cup
- Tofu pieces, one pound
- Minced garlic, two tablespoon
- Minced ginger, two tablespoon
- Cilantro, half cup
- Olive oil, two tablespoon
- Chopped tomatoes, one cup

- Cooked noodles, two cup

Instructions:

1. Take a pan.

2. Add in the oil and onions.

3. Cook the onions until they become soft and fragrant.

4. Add in the chopped garlic and ginger.

5. Cook the mixture and add the tomatoes into it.

6. Add the spices.

7. When the tomatoes are done, add the tofu pieces into it.

8. Mix the ingredients carefully.

9. Bake the tofu cubes for fifteen minutes.

10. When your tofu is done, mix it with the noodles.

11. Add in the cilantro.

12. Your dish is ready to be served.

3.6 Vegetarian Thai Curry Fettucini Recipe

Preparation Time: 30 minutes

Cooking Time: 10 minutes

Serving: 4

Ingredients:

- Water, two cups
- Rice noodles, one pack
- Galangal, one can
- Minced garlic, one teaspoon
- Minced ginger, one teaspoon
- Chopped onion, half cup
- Minced ginger, half tablespoon
- Lemon grass, two sticks
- Fish sauce, two tablespoon
- Coconut milk, one cup
- Cilantro, a quarter cup
- Olive oil, one tablespoon

Instructions:

1. Take a large sauce wok.
2. Add the chopped onion and olive oil.
3. Cook your chopped onion.
4. When the onions are cooked then add the galangal, minced garlic and ginger.
5. Add the coconut milk.
6. Cook your ingredients until they start boiling.
7. Add in the lemon grass and rest of the ingredients into your curry.
8. Now add the water and noodles into the dish.
9. Cook your ingredients for ten minutes.

10.   Garnish it with cilantro leaves.

11.   Your dish is ready to be served.

3.7 Vegetarian Thai Basil Fried Rice Recipe

Preparation Time: 30 minutes

Cooking Time: 10 minutes

Serving: 4

Ingredients:

- Thai fresh basil leaves, one cup
- Sliced green onions, half cup
- White peppercorns, one teaspoon
- Cilantro, one cup
- Fresh ginger, one teaspoon
- Fish sauce, one tablespoon
- Soy sauce, one tablespoon
- Chili garlic sauce, two tablespoon
- Fresh cilantro leaves, half cup
- Cooked rice, as required

Instructions:

1. Heat a large pan.

2. Add the vegetable broth and sauces into the mixture.

3. Cook your dish for ten minutes.

4. Add the cooked rice into the mixture.

5. Mix the rice well and cook it for five minutes.

6. Add the rest of the ingredients into the mixture.

7. Cook your dish for five more minutes.

8. Add the basil leaves and cilantro into the dish.

9. Mix your rice and then dish it out.

10. Your dish is ready to be served.

3.8 Vegetarian Thai Butternut Squash and Chickpea Curry Recipe

Preparation Time: 30 minutes

Cooking Time: 10 minutes

Serving: 4

Ingredients:

- Cooked chickpeas, two cup

- Vegetable stock, two cups
- Minced garlic, one teaspoon
- Thai spices, two tablespoon
- Shallot, one
- Kaffir lime leaves, four
- Lime wedges
- Lemon grass, two sticks
- Fish sauce, two tablespoon
- Coconut milk, one cup
- Cilantro, a quarter cup
- Butternut squash pieces, half pound
- Olive oil, one tablespoon

Instructions:

1. Take a large sauce pan.
2. Add the shallots and olive oil.
3. Cook your shallots and then add the butternut squash pieces.
4. When the butternut squash pieces are half cooked, add the galangal, vegetable stock, and minced garlic.
5. Add the cooked chickpeas into your curry.
6. Add the coconut milk and the rest of the ingredients.
7. Cook your ingredients for ten minutes.

8. Garnish it with cilantro leaves.

9. Your dish is ready to be served.

3.9 Vegetarian Thai Creamy Peanut Ramen Recipe

Preparation Time: 30 minutes

Cooking Time: 10 minutes

Serving: 4

Ingredients:

- Coconut cream, one cup
- Sliced green onions, half cup
- White peppercorns, one teaspoon
- Cilantro, one cup
- Fresh ginger, one teaspoon
- Fish sauce, one tablespoon
- Soy sauce, one tablespoon
- Chinese 5 spice, half teaspoon
- Chili garlic sauce, two tablespoon
- Fresh cilantro leaves, half cup
- Peanuts, two cups
- Minced lemon grass, one teaspoon
- Ramen, as required

Instructions:

1. Add all the ingredients of the sauce into a pan.

2. Add the coconut cream and the rest of the ingredients into the mixture.

3. Cook your dish for ten minutes.

4. Add the ramen into the mixture once the sauce is ready.

5. Mix the ramen well and cook it for five minutes.

6. Add the peanuts into the pan.

7. Cook your dish for five more minutes.

8. Add the cilantro into the dish.

9. Your dish is ready to be served.

3.10 Vegetarian Thai Chickpea and Sweet Potato Curry Recipe

Preparation Time: 30 minutes

Cooking Time: 10 minutes

Serving: 4

Ingredients

- Cooked chickpeas, two cup
- Vegetable stock, two cups
- Minced garlic, one teaspoon
- Thai spices, two tablespoon

- Shallot, one
- Kaffir lime leaves, four
- Lime wedges
- Lemon grass, two sticks
- Fish sauce, two tablespoon
- Coconut milk, one cup
- Cilantro, a quarter cup
- Sweet potato pieces, half pound
- Olive oil, one tablespoon

Instructions:

1. Take a large sauce pan.
2. Add the shallots and olive oil.
3. Cook your shallots and then add the sweet potato pieces.
4. When the sweet potato pieces are half cooked, add the galangal, vegetable stock, and minced garlic.
5. Add the cooked chickpeas into your curry.
6. Add the coconut milk and the rest of the ingredients.
7. Cook your ingredients for ten minutes.
8. Garnish it with cilantro leaves.
9. Your dish is ready to be served.

3.11 Vegetarian Thai Pineapple Rice Recipe

Preparation Time: 30 minutes

Cooking Time: 10 minutes

Serving: 4

Ingredients:

- Chopped pineapple pieces, one cup
- Sliced green onions, half cup
- White peppercorns, one teaspoon
- Cilantro, one cup
- Fresh ginger, one teaspoon
- Fish sauce, one tablespoon
- Soy sauce, one tablespoon
- Chili garlic sauce, two tablespoon
- Fresh cilantro leaves, half cup
- Cooked rice, as required

Instructions:

1. Heat a large pan.
2. Add the vegetable broth and sauces into the mixture.
3. Cook your dish for ten minutes.
4. Add the cooked rice into the mixture.
5. Mix the rice well and cook it for five minutes.
6. Add the rest of the ingredients into the mixture.
7. Cook your dish for five more minutes.
8. Add the chopped pineapple and cilantro into the dish.
9. Mix your rice and then dish it out.

10.   Your dish is ready to be served.

3.12 Vegetarian Thai Tofu and Pepper Eggplant Recipe

Preparation Time: 30 minutes

Cooking Time: 10 minutes

Serving: 4

Ingredients:

- Eggplant cubes, two cups
- Red bell pepper, one cup
- Yellow bell pepper, one cup
- Green bell pepper, one cup
- Sliced green onions, half cup
- White peppercorns, one teaspoon
- Cilantro, one cup

- Fresh ginger, one teaspoon

- Fish sauce, one tablespoon

- Soy sauce, one tablespoon

- Chili paste, one tablespoon

- Tofu cubes, two cup

- Chili garlic sauce, two tablespoon

- Fresh cilantro leaves, half cup

- Fresh basil leaves, a quarter cup

- Vegetable broth, one cup

Instructions:

1. Add all the ingredients of the sauce into a wok.

2. Add the chili paste, eggplant, bell peppers, vegetable broth and sauces into the mixture.

3. Cook your dish for ten minutes.

4. Add the tofu cubes and the rest of the ingredients into the mixture once the sauce is ready.

5. Mix the tofu cubes well and cook them for five minutes.

6. Add the cilantro into the dish.

7. Your dish is ready to be served.

3.13 Vegetarian Thai Baby Corn and Vegetables Stir-Fry Recipe

Preparation Time: 10 minutes

Cooking Time: 20 minutes

Ingredients:

- Fish sauce, two tablespoon
- Soy sauce, half cup
- Tomatoes, two
- Baby corn, two cups
- Cilantro, half cup
- Salt and pepper, to taste
- Minced ginger, half tablespoon
- Vegetable oil, two tablespoon
- Red chili peppers, three
- Onion, one
- Mixed vegetables, one cup
- Scallions, half cup
- Minced garlic, one teaspoon

Instructions:

1. In a large wok, add the shallots and oil.
2. Cook the shallots and then add the ginger and garlic.
3. Cook the ginger and garlic.
4. Add the mixed vegetables, baby corn and the rest of the ingredients into your dish except the toasted nuts.

5. Cook your dish for five minutes.

6. Garnish your dish with cilantro.

7. Your dish is ready to be served.

3.14 Vegetarian Thai Tofu and Coconut Curry Recipe

Preparation Time: 30 minutes

Cooking Time: 10 minutes

Serving: 4

Ingredients:

- Unsweetened shredded coconut, one cup
- Vegetable stock, two cups
- Minced garlic, one teaspoon
- Thai spices, two tablespoon
- Shallot, one
- Galangal, half teaspoon
- Mixed vegetables, half cup
- Kaffir lime leaves, four

- Lemon grass, two sticks
- Fish sauce, two tablespoon
- Coconut milk, one cup
- Cilantro, a quarter cup
- Tofu cubes, half pound
- Olive oil, one tablespoon

Instructions:

1. Take a large sauce pan.
2. Add the shallots and olive oil.
3. Cook your shallots and then add the vegetables and tofu cubes.
4. Add the galangal, vegetable stock, and minced garlic.
5. Add the coconut milk.
6. Add the unsweetened shredded coconut and the rest of the ingredients.
7. Cook your ingredients for ten minutes.
8. Garnish it with cilantro leaves.
9. Your dish is ready to be served.

3.15 Vegetarian Thai Lentils in Peanut Sauce Recipe

Preparation Time: 30 minutes

Cooking Time: 10 minutes

Serving: 4

Ingredients:

- Mixed lentils, two cups
- Minced garlic, one teaspoon
- Minced ginger, one teaspoon
- Chopped onion, half cup
- Minced ginger, half tablespoon
- Lemon grass, two sticks
- Fish sauce, two tablespoon
- Spicy peanut sauce, one cup
- Coconut milk, one cup
- Cilantro, a quarter cup
- Olive oil, one tablespoon

Instructions:

1. Take a large sauce pan.
2. Add the chopped onion and olive oil.
3. Cook your chopped onion and then add the lentils.
4. Add the coconut milk.
5. Cook your ingredients until they start boiling.
6. Add in the spicy peanut sauce and the rest of the ingredients.
7. Cook your ingredients for ten minutes.
8. Garnish it with cilantro leaves.
9. Your dish is ready to be served.

3.16 Vegetarian Thai Black Pepper and Garlic Tofu Recipe

Preparation Time: 30 minutes

Cooking Time: 20 minutes

Serving: 4

Ingredients:

- Minced garlic, two tablespoon
- Minced ginger, two tablespoon
- Cilantro, half cup
- Olive oil, two tablespoon
- Chopped tomatoes, one cup
- Powdered cumin, one tablespoon
- Salt, to taste
- Black pepper, two tablespoon
- Turmeric powder, one teaspoon
- Onion, one cup
- Vegetable broth, one cup
- Smoked paprika, half teaspoon
- Water, half cup
- Tofu cubes, one pound

Instructions:

1. Take a wok.

2. Add in the oil and onions.

3. Cook the onions until they become soft and fragrant.

4. Add in the chopped garlic and ginger.

5. Cook the mixture and add the tomatoes into it.

6. Add the spices.

7. When the tomatoes are done, add the tofu cubes into it.

8. Mix the tofu so that the tomatoes and spices are coated all over the tofu.

9. Cook for five minutes.

10. Add in the water.

11. Mix the ingredients carefully and cover your wok.

12. When your tofu is done, add in the cilantro.

13. Your dish is ready to be served.

3.17 Vegetarian Thai Panang Curry with Vegetables Recipe

Preparation Time: 30 minutes

Cooking Time: 10 minutes

Serving: 4

Ingredients:

- Panang curry paste, two tablespoon

- Vegetable stock, two cups
- Minced garlic, one teaspoon
- Thai spices, two tablespoon
- Shallot, one
- Galangal, half teaspoon
- Kaffir lime leaves, four
- Lemon grass, two sticks
- Fish sauce, two tablespoon
- Coconut milk, one cup
- Cilantro, a quarter cup
- Mixed vegetables, half pound
- Olive oil, one tablespoon

Instructions:

1. Take a large sauce pan.
2. Add the shallots and olive oil.
3. Cook your shallots and then add the mixed vegetables.
4. Add the galangal, vegetable stock, and minced garlic.
5. Add the coconut milk and pananag curry paste.
6. Add the rest of the ingredients.
7. Cook your ingredients for ten minutes.
8. Garnish it with cilantro leaves.
9. Your dish is ready to be served.

3.18 Vegetarian Thai Tofu in Peanut Butter Sauce Recipe

Preparation Time: 30 minutes

Cooking Time: 10 minutes

Serving: 4

Ingredients:

- Tofu cubes, two cups
- Minced garlic, one teaspoon
- Minced ginger, one teaspoon
- Chopped onion, half cup
- Minced ginger, half tablespoon
- Lemon grass, two sticks
- Fish sauce, two tablespoon
- Peanut butter sauce, one cup
- Coconut milk, one cup
- Cilantro, a quarter cup
- Olive oil, one tablespoon

Instructions:

1. Take a large sauce pan.
2. Add the chopped onion and olive oil.
3. Cook your chopped onion and then add the tofu.
4. Add the coconut milk.
5. Cook your ingredients until they start boiling.
6. Add in the peanut butter sauce and the rest of the ingredients.
7. Cook your ingredients for ten minutes.
8. Garnish it with cilantro leaves.
9. Your dish is ready to be served.

Chapter 4: The World of Vegetarian Thai Dessert

This chapter focuses on healthy Thai vegetarian dessert recipes that you will find very easy to make on your own.

4.1 Vegetarian Thai Caramelized Coconut Cake Recipe

Preparation Time: 10 minutes

Cooking Time: 20 minutes

Serving: 4

Ingredients:

- Coconut milk, one cup
- Coconut flakes, half cup
- Baking powder, four teaspoon
- Eggs, two
- Whole wheat flour, half cup
- Baking soda, one teaspoon
- Rice flour, one cup
- Sugar, half cup
- Vanilla extract, one tablespoon

Instructions:

1. In a large bowl, add the eggs.

2. Beat the eggs until they turn creamy and frothy.

3. Add the melted butter and coconut milk into the mixture.

4. Add the sugar and beat the mixture for five more minutes.

5. In a separate bowl, add all the dried ingredients.

6. Slowly add your dried mixture into your wet mixture.

7. Add the vanilla extract as required.

8. Bake your cake for ten to fifteen minutes.

9. When done, dish it out on a rack.

10. Your dish is ready to be served.

4.2 Vegetarian Thai Mango Dessert Recipe

Preparation Time: 10 minutes

Cooking Time: 20 minutes

Serving: 4

Ingredients:

- Sliced mangoes, one cup

- Rice, one cup

- Baking powder, four teaspoon

- Coconut milk, one cup

- All-purpose flour, one and a half cup

- Baking soda, one teaspoon

- Eggs, two

- Brown sugar, one cup

- Tapioca starch, one tablespoon

- Salt, to taste

Instructions:

1. In a large bowl, add the eggs.
2. Beat the eggs until they turn frothy.
3. Add the baking powder and coconut milk into it.
4. Add the brown sugar and beat the mixture for five more minutes.
5. In a separate bowl, add all the dried ingredients.
6. Mix them thoroughly.
7. Cook the rice in rice cooking pan.
8. Add the salt and pepper as required.
9. Put the mango slices on cooked rice.
10. Your dish is ready to be served.

4.3 Vegetarian Thai Mung Bean Pudding Recipe

Preparation Time: 10 minutes

Cooking Time: 20 minutes

Serving: 4

Ingredients:

- Mung beans, one cup
- Baking powder, four teaspoon
- Barley flakes, one and a half cup
- Baking soda, one teaspoon
- Buttermilk, two cups
- White sugar, one cup
- Water, two cups
- Tapioca flour, one cup
- Coconut cream, half cup

Instructions:

1. In a large bowl, add the tapioca flour into it.
2. Add the mung beans into the mixture.
3. Add the white sugar and beat the mixture for five more minutes.
4. In a separate bowl, add all the dried ingredients.
5. Add the water into it
6. Add the coconut cream into the mixture.
7. Mix them thoroughly until a homogeneous mixture is obtained.
8. Check the thickness of pudding and add sugar and flour if required.
9. Your dish is ready to be served.

4.4 Vegetarian Thai Coconut Black Rice Pudding Recipe

Preparation Time: 20 minutes

Cooking Time: 20 minutes

Serving: 4

Ingredients:

- Cooked black rice, one bowl
- Cilantro, as required
- Baking powder, four teaspoon
- Coconut flakes, one and a half cup
- Baking soda, one teaspoon
- Buttermilk, two cups
- White sugar, one cup
- Water, two cups
- Tapioca flour, one cup
- Coconut cream, half cup

Instructions:

1. In a large bowl, add the tapioca flour into it.
2. Add the white sugar into the mixture as required.

3. Add the baking powder and beat the mixture for five more minutes.

4. In a separate bowl, add the water in it.

5. Add coconut flakes into it.

6. Add the coconut cream into the mixture.

7. Add the cooked rice into it.

8. Mix them thoroughly until a consistent mixture is formed.

9. Check the thickness of pudding and add sugar and flour if required.

10. Your dish is ready to be served.

4.5 Vegetarian Thai Sticky Banana Rice Recipe

Preparation Time: 10 minutes

Cooking Time: 20 minutes

Serving: 4

Ingredients:

- Sweet rice, two cup
- Banana leaves, five
- Bananas, five
- Salt, a pinch
- Bread flour, half cup
- Coconut milk, one cup
- Lime zest, as required

- Pepper, to taste
- Soy sauce, one tablespoon

Instructions:

1. In a large bowl, add the bread flour into it.
2. Cook the rice in the rice cooking pan.
3. Add the rice into it and mix them.
4. Add the lime zest as required.
5. Add the cilantro if required.
6. Add the banana leaves into the mixture.
7. Add the banana pieces into it.
8. Add some water and boil the whole mixture for ten minutes.
9. Your dish is ready to be served.

4.6 Thai Bananas in Coconut Milk Recipe

Preparation Time: 10 minutes

Cooking Time: 20 minutes

Serving: 4

Ingredients:

- Coconut milk, one cup
- Bananas, five
- Salt, a pinch
- Bread flour, half cup
- Coconut milk, one cup
- Lime zest, as required
- Pepper, to taste
- Brown sugar, two tablespoon

Instructions:

1. Heat a large pan.
2. Take a bowl and add the coconut milk into it.
3. Add the banana pieces into it.
4. Add the lime zest as required.
5. Add the cilantro and rest of the ingredients if required.
6. Add the mixture into the pan.
7. Add some water and simmer the whole mixture for ten minutes.
8. Your dish is ready to be served.

4.7 Thai Mung Bean Sweets Recipe

Preparation Time: 10 minutes

Cooking Time: 20 minutes

Serving: 4

Ingredients:

- Mung beans, one cup
- Baking powder, four teaspoon
- Barley flakes, one and a half cup
- Baking soda, one teaspoon
- Buttermilk, two cups
- White sugar, one cup
- Water, two cups
- Tapioca flour, one cup
- Coconut cream, half cup

Instructions:

1. In a large bowl, add the tapioca flour into it.
2. Add the mung beans into the mixture.
3. Add the white sugar and beat the mixture for five more minutes.
4. In a separate bowl, add all the dried ingredients.
5. Add the water into it.
6. Add the coconut cream into the mixture.
7. Mix them thoroughly until a consistent mixture is formed.
8. Cook your mixture until it thickens.
9. Switch off the stove.

10. Make small round structures from the mixture.

11. Your dish is ready to be served.

4.8 Thai Mango and Coconut Sauce Recipe

Preparation Time: 10 minutes

Cooking Time: 20 minutes

Serving: 4

Ingredients:

- Sliced mangoes, one cup
- Coconut milk, one cup
- Lime zest, as required
- Red bell pepper, one tablespoon
- Pepper, to taste
- Salt, to taste

Instructions:

1. Take a bowl and add the coconut milk into it.
2. Add the lime zest into it.
3. Add the salt and pepper as required.
4. Add the cilantro if required.
5. In the end, add the Mango slices into the mixture.
6. Boil the whole mixture for ten minutes
7. Your dish is ready to be served.

4.9 Thai Rice Balls in Coconut Milk Recipe

Preparation Time: 10 minutes

Cooking Time: 20 minutes

Serving: 4

Ingredients:

- Coconut milk, one cup
- Rice balls, one cup
- Salt, a pinch
- Bread flour, half cup
- Coconut milk, one cup
- Lime zest, as required
- Pepper, to taste
- Brown sugar, two tablespoon

Instructions:

1. Heat a large pan.
2. Take a bowl and add the coconut milk into it.
3. Add the rice balls into it.
4. Add the lime zest as required.
5. Add the cilantro and rest of the ingredients if required.
6. Add the mixture into the pan.

7. Add some water and simmer the whole mixture for ten minutes.

8. Your dish is ready to be served.

4.10 Thai Coconut Balls Recipe

Preparation Time: 10 minutes

Cooking Time: 10 minutes

Serving: 4

Ingredients:

- Glutinous rice flour, three cups
- Sweetened shredded coconut, a quarter cup
- Vegetable oil, two tablespoon
- Brown sugar, two cups
- Coconut milk, a quarter cup
- Sweetened red bean paste, one cup

Instructions:

1. Heat a wok.
2. Add the vegetable oil in the wok.
3. Add the sweetened shredded coconut.
4. Cook them for five minutes.
5. Add the glutinous rice flour and brown sugar into the wok.
6. Add the coconut milk and sweetened red bean paste into the mixture.

7. Cook your dish and then dish it out.

8. When the mixture turns a little cold, make small round balls from the mixture.

9. Your dish is ready to be served.

4.11 Thai Style Crème Caramel Recipe

Preparation Time: 10 minutes

Cooking Time: 30 minutes

Serving: 6

Ingredients:
- Palm sugar, half cup
- Eggs, four
- Caster sugar, two cups
- Vanilla essence, one teaspoon
- Coconut milk, one cup

Instructions:
1. Take a large bowl.
2. Add the eggs into the bowl.
3. Beat the eggs well.
4. When they turn fluffy, add the palm sugar into it and beat the mixture well.
5. Make sure your sugar dissolves into the mixture.
6. Add the vanilla essence and coconut milk into the mixture.

7. Add the mixture in non-stick mold.

8. Bake your mixture for ten minutes.

9. Dish out and sprinkle the caster sugar on top.

10.   Your dish is ready to be served.

4.12 Thai Fried Banana Rolls Recipe

Preparation Time: 10 minutes

Cooking Time: 10 minutes

Serving: 2

Ingredients:

- Chopped bananas, five
- Shredded coconut, half cup
- Wonton wraps, as required
- Chinese five spice, as needed
- Cooking oil, as required

Instructions:

1. In a large bowl, mix all the ingredients together.

2. Add the mixture into the wonton wrappers.

3. Wrap your rolls.

4. Fry your rolls until they turn golden brown.

5. Dish out and drizzle any sauce if you want on top.

6. Your dish is ready to be served.

4.13 Thai Sticky Rice Cake Recipe

Preparation Time: 10 minutes

Cooking Time: 20 minutes

Serving: 4

Ingredients:

- Sweet rice, two cups
- Banana leaves, five
- Bananas, five
- Salt, a pinch
- Bread flour, half cup
- Coconut milk, one cup
- Lime zest, as required
- Pepper, to taste
- Baking powder, one teaspoon
- Vanilla essence, half teaspoon
- Soy sauce, one tablespoon

Instructions:

1. In a large bowl, add the bread flour into it.
2. Cook the rice in the rice cooking pan.
3. Add the rice into it and mix them.
4. Add the lime zest as required.

5. Add the cilantro if required.

6. Add the banana leaves into the mixture.

7. Add the banana pieces into it.

8. Add some water and boil the whole mixture for ten minutes.

9. Cool your mixture and then add the vanilla essence, baking powder and coconut milk into it.

10.   Mix your ingredients.

11.   Bake your rice cake.

12.   When your cake is done, dish it out and slice it up.

13.   Your dish is ready to be served.

4.14 Thai Mangosteen Custard Recipe

Preparation Time: 30 minutes

Cooking Time: 10 minutes

Serving: 4

Ingredients:

- Mangosteen cubes, one cup

- Eggs, two

- Coconut, two

- Chinese sweet spices, to taste

- Coconut milk, half cup

- White sugar, half cup

- Salt, one teaspoon

- Lemon extract, one teaspoon

- Almond extract, one teaspoon

- All-purpose flour, two cups

- Butter, one cup

Instructions:

1. Take a medium bowl and add the eggs and the tapioca flour in it.

2. Add one cup of coconut milk and mix well.

3. Add the sugar, salt and the beaten eggs.

4. Mix them well.

5. Mix the warm milk mixture with the flour and the coconut.

6. Add the eggs, lemon extract and almond extract together.

7. Add the baking soda in the mixture.

8. Simmer it for few minutes.

9. Add the mangosteen cubes in the end.

10. Check the thickness of the custard.

11. Your dish is ready to be served.

4.15 Thai Mango Layered Custard Recipe

Preparation Time: 30 minutes

Cooking Time: 10 minutes

Serving: 4

Ingredients:

- Mango cubes, one cup
- Eggs, two
- Coconut, two
- Chinese sweet spices, to taste
- Coconut milk, half cup
- White sugar, half cup
- Salt, one teaspoon
- Lemon extract, one teaspoon
- Almond extract, one teaspoon
- All-purpose flour, two cups
- Butter, one cup

Instructions:

1. Take a medium bowl and add the eggs and the tapioca flour in it.

2. Add the one cup coconut milk and mix well.

3. Add the sugar, salt and the beaten eggs.

4. Mix them well.

5. Mix the warm milk mixture with the flour and the coconut.

6. Add the eggs, lemon extract and almond extract together.

7. Add the baking soda in the mixture.

8. Simmer it for a few minutes.

9. Check the thickness of the custard.

10.   In a large bowl, spread some of the custard mixture in the end.

11.   Add a layer of the mongo cubes.

12.   Add a layer of the custard again.

13.   Complete your layered custard.

14.   Your dish is ready to be served.

Chapter 5: The World of Vegetarian Thai Snack Recipes

Following are some classic vegetarian Thai snack recipes that are rich in healthy nutrients and you can easily make them with the detailed instructions list in each recipe:

5.1 Vegetarian Thai Peanut Cauliflower Wings Recipe

Preparation Time: 10 minutes

Cooking Time: 20 minutes

Serving: 4

Ingredients:

- Cauliflower florets, one cup
- Flour, one cup
- Almond milk, one cup
- Garlic powder, one tablespoon
- Peanut butter, one cup
- Soy sauce, one tablespoon
- Sesame oil, one tablespoon
- Lime juice, one tablespoon
- Coconut sugar, two teaspoon

- Ginger, one tablespoon
- Water, two cups
- Sesame seeds, for topping
- Green onion, for topping

Instructions:

1. Take a bowl and add the flour in it.
2. Add the almond milk and garlic powder.
3. Mix them thoroughly.
4. Then add salt and pepper as required.
5. Take a baking pan and add the cauliflower florets into it.
6. Bake it for twenty minutes.
7. Mix the sauce ingredients in a bowl.
8. Mix the sauce and cauliflower in a bowl together.
9. Use sesame seeds and the green onions for topping.
10. Your dish is ready to be served.

5.2 Vegetarian Thai Cabbage Salad Recipe

Preparation Time: 10 minutes

Cooking Time: 25 minutes

Serving: 4

Ingredients:

- Sesame seeds, as required
- Shredded red cabbage, two cups
- Carrot sliced, one cup
- Red bell pepper sliced, one cup
- Chopped mango, half cup
- Green onion, half cup
- Coriander leaves, half cup
- Thai red chili, half cup
- Peanut butter, two tablespoon
- Lime juice, one tablespoon
- Ginger, one tablespoon
- Garlic powder, two teaspoon
- Maple syrup, half teaspoon
- Sesame oil, one teaspoon
- Soy sauce, one teaspoon
- Sriracha, one tablespoon
- Salt, to taste
- Pepper, to taste

Instructions:

1. Take a large bowl and add all the vegetables one by one

2. Add the ginger and garlic powder.

3. Mix well.

4. Add the peanuts and mix gently

5. Add lime juice, maple syrup, Thai red chili and soy sauce.

6. Add the salt and pepper as you like.

7. Add the sesame oil and sesame seeds and mix well.

8. Add the sriracha into the mixture.

9. Mix all ingredients and make good combination.

10. Your salad is ready to be served.

5.3 Vegetarian Thai Slow with Ginger Peanut Dressing Recipe

Preparation Time: 30 minutes

Cooking Time: 25 minutes

Serving: 4

Ingredients:

- Ginger, two tablespoon

- Peanuts, one cup

- Carrot sliced, one cup

- Red bell pepper sliced, one cup

- Green onion, half cup

- Coriander leaves, half cup

- Thai red chili, half cup

- Peanut butter, two tablespoon

- Lime juice, one tablespoon

- Ginger, one tablespoon

- Garlic powder, two teaspoon

- Maple syrup, half teaspoon

- Sesame oil, one teaspoon

- Salt, to taste

- Pepper, to taste

Instructions:

1. Take a large bowl and add all the vegetables one by one.

2. Add the ginger and garlic powder.

3. Mix well until a good mixture is obtained.

4. Add the peanuts and mix gently.

5. Add lime juice, maple syrup, Thai red chili and soy sauce.

6. Add the salt and pepper as you like.

7. Add the maple syrup, red bell peppers and peanut butter.

8. Add the sriracha into the mixture.

9. Mix all ingredients and pour the ginger and the peanuts on top.

10. Your salad is ready to be served.

5.4 Vegetarian Thai Chickpea Salad with Curry Peanut Dressing Recipe

Preparation Time: 20 minutes

Cooking Time: 20 minutes

Serving: 4

Ingredients:

- Chickpea, one bowl
- Curry Peanuts, one cup
- Carrot sliced, one cup
- Red bell pepper sliced, one cup
- Green onion, half cup
- Coriander leaves, half cup
- Thai red chili, half cup
- Peanut butter, two tablespoon
- Lime juice, one tablespoon
- Ginger, one tablespoon
- Garlic powder, two teaspoon
- Maple syrup, half teaspoon
- Sesame oil, one teaspoon
- Salt, to taste
- Pepper, to taste

Instructions:

1. Take a large bowl and add all the vegetables one by one.

2. Add the ginger and garlic powder to it.

3. Mix well until a good mixture is obtained.

4. Add the peanuts and mix gently

5. Add lime juice, maple syrup, Thai red chili and soy sauce.

6. Add the salt and pepper as you like.

7. Add the maple syrup, red bell peppers and peanut butter.

8. Add the sriracha into the mixture.

9. Mix all ingredients and pour the chickpea and curry peanut on the top.

10. Your salad is ready to be served.

5.5 Vegetarian Thai Kale and Cabbage Salad Recipe

Preparation Time: 20 minutes

Cooking Time: 20 minutes

Serving: 2

Ingredients:

- Cabbage, one cup
- Thai kale, one cup
- Carrot sliced, one cup
- Red bell pepper sliced, one cup
- Green onion, half cup

- Coriander leaves, half cup

- Thai red chili, half cup

- Peanut butter, two tablespoon

- Lime juice, one tablespoon

- Ginger, one tablespoon

- Garlic powder, two teaspoon

- Maple syrup, half teaspoon

- Sesame oil, one teaspoon

- Salt, to taste

- Pepper, to taste

Instructions:

1. Take a large bowl and add all the vegetables one by one.
2. Add the ginger and garlic powder to it.
3. Mix well until a good mixture is formed.
4. Add the peanuts and mix gently.
5. Add lime juice, maple syrup, Thai red chili and soy sauce.
6. Add the salt and pepper as you like.
7. Add the maple syrup, red bell peppers and peanut butter.
8. Add the sriracha into the mixture.
9. Add the kale slices and cabbage into the mixture.
10. Your salad is ready to be served.

5.6 Vegetarian Thai Peanuts and Noodles Salad Recipe

Preparation Time: 10 minutes

Cooking Time: 20 minutes

Serving: 4

Ingredients:

- Peanuts, one cup
- Noodles, one pack
- Carrot sliced, one cup
- Red bell pepper sliced, one cup
- Green onion, half cup
- Coriander leaves, half cup
- Thai red chili, half cup
- Peanut butter, two tablespoon
- Lime juice, one tablespoon
- Ginger, one tablespoon
- Garlic powder, two teaspoon
- Maple syrup, half teaspoon
- Sesame oil, one teaspoon
- Salt, to taste
- Pepper, to taste

Instructions:

1. Take a large bowl and add the boiling water into it.

2. Prepare noodles in it for five minutes.

3. Add the ginger and garlic powder to it.

4. Mix well until a good mixture is obtained.

5. Add the peanuts and mix gently.

6. Add lime juice, maple syrup, Thai red chili and soy sauce.

7. Add the salt and pepper as you like.

8. Add the maple syrup, red bell peppers and peanut butter.

9. Add the noodles into the mixture.

10. Your salad is ready to be served.

5.7 Vegetarian Thai Satay Rolls Recipe

Preparation Time: 30 minutes

Cooking Time: 25 minutes

Serving: 4

Ingredients:

- Baby arugula, one cup
- Cilantro, one
- Red bell pepper, one tablespoon
- Cucumber, two

- Peanut butter, half cup
- Coconut milk, one cup
- Garlic powder, two tablespoon
- Ginger, one tablespoon
- Soy sauce, one tablespoon
- Lime juice, one tablespoon
- Brown sugar, two tablespoon

Instructions:

1. Heat the water in a pan.
2. Dip the rice paper into the warm water.
3. Add the cilantro, mint, bell pepper and cucumbers into it.
4. Add the peanut butter, coconut milk into it.
5. Add the ginger and the garlic powder as required.
6. Add the brown sugar as required.
7. Season it with the salt and pepper.
8. Tightly roll the rice paper over all the ingredients.
9. Serve the rolls with soy sauce.

5.8 Vegetarian Thai Corn and Zucchini Fritters Recipe

Preparation Time: 30 minutes

Cooking Time: 5 minutes

Serving: 4

Ingredients:

- All-purpose flour, one cup
- Fresh corn, half cup
- Baking powder, one cup
- Cumin, half tablespoon
- Salt, one tablespoon
- Milk, one cup
- Black pepper, one tablespoon
- Eggs, two
- Butter, half cup
- Oil, one cup

Instructions:

1. Take a large bowl and add the flour into it.
2. Add the sugar, salt, the pepper and cumin.
3. Mix them well.
4. Take another bowl and add the eggs and milk into it.
5. Add the butter and mix the ingredients.

6. Stir it in the zucchini, corn and cheese.

7. Mix them thoroughly.

8. Warm the oil in the skillet.

9. Fry the mixture until it becomes brown and crispy.

10.   Your dish is ready to be served.

5.9 Vegetarian Thai Curry Tacos Recipe

Preparation Time: 30 minutes

Cooking Time: 10 minutes

Serving: 4

Ingredients:

- Thai red curry paste, two tablespoon
- Canola oil, one cup
- Minced garlic, two tablespoon
- Chopped red onion, one cup
- Coconut milk, one cup
- Lime juice, two tablespoon
- Water, as required
- Cilantro leaves, as required
- Salt, a pinch
- Taco shells, as required
- Avocado sliced, two

Instructions:

1. Add the canola oil into the skillet.
2. Add the curry paste and garlic powder.
3. Cook it for five minutes.
4. Add more oil into it and add all the ingredients.
5. Add the salt and pepper as required.
6. Cook it for few minutes more.
7. Add the ingredients into the taco shells.
8. Your dish is ready to be served.

5.10 Spicy Vegetarian Thai Grapefruit Salad Recipe

Preparation Time: 30 minutes

Cooking Time: 50 minutes

Serving: 5

Ingredients:

- Grape fruits, one cup
- Tomatoes, one or two
- Carrot sliced, one cup
- Red bell pepper sliced, one cup
- Green onion, half cup
- Coriander leaves, half cup

- Thai red chili, half cup

- Peanut butter, two tablespoon

- Lime juice, one tablespoon

- Ginger, one tablespoon

- Garlic powder, two teaspoon

- Maple syrup, half teaspoon

- Sesame oil, one teaspoon

- Salt, to taste

- Pepper, to taste

Instructions:

1. Take a large bowl and add the peeled grapefruit and the vegetables one by one.
2. Add the ginger and garlic powder to it.
3. Mix well until a good mixture is formed.
4. Add the peanuts and mix gently
5. Add lime juice, maple syrup, Thai red chili and soy sauce.
6. Add the salt and pepper as you like.
7. Add the maple syrup, red bell peppers and peanut butter.
8. Add the sriracha into the mixture.
9. Mix all ingredients well so that a homogeneous mixture is obtained.
10. Your salad is ready to be served.

Conclusion

Thailand is the most acclaimed nation in the whole world for its cooking. Traversing from the southern landmass toward the northern regions, the nation offers a various mix of madly flavorful food. Thai food is not the only cuisine to have been changed in the excursion across seas. Various vegetarian Thai foods are loved across the world and you in particular would enjoy cooking your vegetarian food with the Thai flavors inserted in them.

The different flavours utilized in Thai cooking have tremendous measure of astounding properties that soundly affects our general wellbeing. This cookbook incorporates 70 healthy plans that contain vegetarian breakfast, vegetarian lunch, vegetarian dinner, vegetarian dessert and vegetarian snack recipes that you can undoubtedly make at home without the help of any kind. Anyway, why order or go out for Thai food when you can be the culinary Thai expert at your home? Start reading and start cooking with this amazing and easy cookbook.